T0374126

MELODY CECELIA HALL - SWOFFORD

TAKING..........
LANESBORO

This book is for
The Lanesboro Burros and the graduating class of
1981
And
In memory of my friend Itchy
and my brother Dave the Rave Hall

ISBN: Softcover   978-1-5144-5937-9
       EBook   978-1-5144-5936-2

Print information available on the last page

Rev. date: 4/15/2019

To order additional copies of this book, contact:
Xlibris
1-888-795-4274
www.Xlibris.com
Orders@Xlibris.com

This book is a humorous look at a simpler time in Lanesboro when it was in its originality based on true stories from the 1970's and the 1980's . Some names and some events have been changed.

Prelude

Port Jefferson was situated along the north shore of Long Island, New York and was a nice place to raise a family, my family. I was a content young lady living there with my four brothers, two sisters, our dogs, cats and monkeys. But In 1974 when I was thirteen years old, my world was turned upside down when my big family and our pets moved from the shores of the east coast to a small Midwestern farm town in Minnesota. The Hall family wasn't ready for Lanesboro and Lanesboro wasn't ready for us! This autobiography will take my readers back to simpler times when Lanesboro was in its originality, with true stories of humor, like chasing escaped monkeys through Sylvan Park and true stories of nostalgia, like experiencing Lanesboro evolve from a tiny, close knit community into the most talked about bed and breakfast town not just in America, but internationally as well. Through these pages I will share with you stories of joy, memories of tears, and mostly some of Lanesboro's legacies and unsung heroes that we must never forget; like the Rank brothers who rid the town of thousands of rattle snakes that caused so much havoc, or the steam engine that roared through town only decades ago, and when Little Norway was considered the quickest route to get to the Oxtrail on foot. Lanesboro is an amazing town now, but was even more amazing then. These true stories should make you giggle and gasp. Enjoy!

Melody C. Hall-Swofford

Melody resides in beautiful Northern Minnesota with her teenage daughter and her three Pomchis. She earned her BA and MA from the College of St. Scholastica and is currently writing Taking Lanesboro II, with more fun to read true life stories about growing up in Lanesboro before it became one of the most popular and most talked about small towns in America. Melody has lived a diversified life and experienced many cultures. She spent the first part of her childhood growing up on the shores of Long Island, New York with her large family, dogs, cats and monkeys. At the age of thirteen she and her family moved to Lanesboro, Minnesota where she learned to appreciate the small town and the beauty of the Midwestern part of the United States. Melody also lived on the California coast for several years and overseas for seven years. She has had the opportunity to experience multi-national cultures which helped to enrich her appreciation for her life-long friends and her home town of Lanesboro. Melody is a ten year veteran with the Army Nurse Corp and the Army Medical Corp and was a devoted army wife for another thirteen years.

CONTENTS

THE FIRST DAY

I screamed at her through the small double paned window as loud as I could. "Heather, Heather stop! We'll be back soon I promise! Stop or you're going to get hurt!" Her jog turned into a fast paced run. As we picked up speed she picked up speed. Heather was running after me and my camper down East Main Street. In fact when she stretched her arms out in front she was just a few feet away from the ladder on the back of the camper. We were only 13 years old but I knew what she was doing was very dangerous. My two brothers and sister were in the station wagon with my parents which was pulling the camper. They were oblivious as to what was going on. I was inside the moving camper with my face and hands pressed against the small bathroom window in the back and I was yelling as loud as I could for her to stop. I'm sure the look of horror on her face mirrored mine when her legs buckled under her fast pace. She almost fell. Heather finally backed off and slowed down. It seemed like she was running after us for more than a mile before she finally gave up. I began to cry as I waved good bye to my best friend, who's image was becoming smaller and smaller right before my very eyes. Our communion had been silenced by the increasing distance and soon she was gone. That was a bittersweet day. That was the day my family moved from Port Jefferson, New York (population 8,000) to Lanesboro, Minnesota.

Port Jefferson was situated along the north shore of Long Island, New York and was a nice place to raise a family. We were a bit of an "eccentric" family, and that was okay in New York. My father was a successful and well known antique dealer and it seemed like he owned half of East Main Street.

The school bus stopped right in front of his main store (he had several) and he was usually there to greet my siblings and I, and often many of my friends like Heather. The kids of the neighborhood called him Uncle Bob and he always had a pocket full of change to give to us so we could run down the street to the candy shop. We lived in Vineyard Place, the last house on the street before the woods. This was a good thing considering the number of kids that would come and go (there were seven of us). The neighbors didn't complain about that as much as they did our pets. We had a lot of cats and dogs and a huge aquarium filled with angel fish, sea horses and many other beautiful salt water fish. What caused the most trouble was our pet monkeys but our neighbors were sort of used to them. Anything goes in New York and exotic pets were the least of oddities. We had wooly monkeys, spider monkeys, capuchins, squirrel monkeys and marmosets (never all at once though). My parents were members of the Simian Society of Long Island and many of the monkeys were rescues. The household was an active one and there was never a boring moment. I was content with my life as a child on the east coast with my brothers, sisters and many pets. With my friends, my big school with an Olympic sized swimming pool and the beach that was only a ten minute walk away from my house. I wasn't ready for a town called Lanesboro and Lanesboro wasn't ready for us.

The year was 1974. Our road trip was turning out to be quite a fiasco and we hadn't even reached the half way mark yet. We were a sight to see traveling down the highway. Shawn our Wooly monkey and Sally our spider monkey accompanied us, as well as four dogs and several cats. My job was to take care of Sally, the dogs and cats in the camper. I didn't mind too much because I could move about when I got restless. Shawn the monkey and Pugsly our little dog were in the station wagon with my siblings and mother and father. The closer we got to Minnesota the more double takes I would notice from people in other vehicles, especially in Iowa and Wisconsin. I guess I would do the same if I was driving down the highway and saw a big black monkey sitting on the lap of the passenger, and then another one peering out the window of a camper being pulled behind. Sally got a few chuckles. She was being good for the most part until she got hungry and decided to help herself into the refrigerator for something to eat while I was taking a nap in the bunk. The sound of jars dropping on the floor woke me up only to see a huge mess of grape jelly, coffee grounds and meal worms spilled all over the tile (people who fish keep night crawlers in their refrigerator and people with monkeys keep meal worms in theirs). The trip took us several days and thank goodness this only happened twice. I managed to get things cleaned up before mother found out. I was supposed to have kept Sally's belt and leash in my hands at all times and under no circumstances was I to let her go. She was a smart monkey and it was a good thing she didn't unlock the outside door while I was napping. We stopped to gas up, change the monkey's diapers and potty the dogs. I was anxious to reach our destination, or should I say destiny. I imagined my brothers and sister felt the same, especially being cooped up in the station wagon for a whole day with the dogs, our wooly monkey Shawn, mom and dad.

As I thought about reaching Lanesboro I became sick to my stomach with anxiety and I wondered if my siblings felt the same. Technically I was a Minnesotan because I was born in Minneapolis, so I was hoping that would be my green card for acceptance from my new friends. When I was about three years old my family moved to Long Island and that was the only way of living I knew. Small farm towns were in books. Corn fields were in scary movies and bulls were in the rodeo. I noticed a lot of horses in Kentucky and sheep in Pennsylvania. There were a lot of stinky pigs in Iowa and herds of cows in Wisconsin, or were they bulls. I couldn't tell the difference because I had never seen a cow or bull before. I imagined the kids in Lanesboro had never seen a monkey either and wouldn't know a squirrel monkey from a marmoset. Heather was used to our monkeys, many dogs and many cats. I missed her so much and wished she was with me, mostly to act as my bodyguard if I needed one. Thirteen is a tough age for any young girl who has to deal with sensationalized emotions, crushes and that first kiss. The most important things to me were my best friend, my clothes and cute boys. I loved my best friend, I loved my clothes and I loved cute boys. I was leaving my 6th grade crush behind with my best friend and that didn't sit too well with me. He looked like Peter Brady and his dad was a doctor. I tried to imagine my first kiss being with a Minnesota farm boy. All I could see in my head was this stereotypical young man wearing bib overalls and a flannel shirt, with a straw hat on his head and a strand of hay sticking out of his mouth, and his name was Jethro. The anxiety was really kicking in now. I wondered how my first day in Lanesboro was going to be. Would my family blend in? Would my new friends like my monkeys? Would I make new friends? Sure I would, I thought. The Midwest can't be too different from the east coast. I thought we probably looked the same and talked the same and wore the same style clothes. After all, my mother grew up in Rochester, Minnesota, but my dad was from the Bronx. He had a very strong accent and a typical New York personality; gregarious, a bit loud and very friendly. My father didn't blend well in Lanesboro and within a few years my parents split up and divorced. It was amiable though. Father wanted all of us to move back to Port Jefferson with him but mother said no. That was that.

MEAL WORMS AND GRAPE JELLY

There are three main highways to enter Lanesboro. By way of Preston which would bring a person into Lanesboro from the edge of town, by way of Rushford which again would gain entrance to Lanesboro from the other edge of town and highway 52, which enters Lanesboro directly in the middle of main street or the middle of town. My father chose highway 52, the grade. Our grand entrance was grand indeed. It just couldn't have happened any other way. I had heard my mother and father discussing the trip and the grade so I knew it must have had some significance to our trip.

Merriam & Webster: /Grade/ Noun. A gradiant or slope, "just over the crest of a long seven percent grade" We traveled highway 52 and passed through Fountain, continuing on until we ran into the grade. By definition, grade means a gradiant or slope which really doesn't sound too bad. This grade however was steep and went on forever. I found out later how the grade had taken a life. Among the many stories my new friends told me about Lanesboro, like the one about the Rank brothers catching thousands of rattle snakes or how the winter hang-out was under the new bridge because it blocked the frigid wind, the story about the grade was the most shocking. I guess back in 1972 a semi-truck was entering Lanesboro by way of the grade. The driver misjudged the steep downhill curve steering right over the cliff and came crashing down near the ball park below. I wish my father would have known this before he chose this route.

When we started to descend pulling our 34 foot camper, with me, my monkey Sally and the dogs in it, things started to roll towards the front. I could tell when my father down shifted into low gear because the camper bucked over and over. The ride was frightening and bumpy. It just so happened that I didn't lock the refrigerator and the door came flying open. Out fell the same unsecured jar of grape jelly, the same unsecured can of coffee grounds spilling into the grape jelly, topped with the container holding the rest of the meal worms that Sally didn't eat. The last time this happened we were traveling down a flat highway and I was able to get it cleaned up before mother saw it, but this time was different. We were only moments away from our new house and any new potential friends. The show was about to begin.

Sally was shrieking while clinging onto me and I was clinging onto the front bunk. I knew the poor monkey was scared half to death because she didn't dive for the meal worms. Meal worms to a monkey are like candy to a child, they are irresistible. The camper bucked a few more times before slowing down and crossing the new bridge which was smack in the middle of Main street, the most active part of this sleepy little town. When we reached the bottom of the bridge at the stop sign, I don't think my father knew whether to turn right or left or go straight because we stopped for what seemed like an eternity and people were starting to take notice. I saw an old couple pass by us. The woman had one hand over her mouth and the other pointing at the car, probably at the big black monkey in a bright blue sweater and wearing a diaper with a hole in it for his tail to go through. Shawn was most likely restless and scared to death as much as Sally! I chuckled because I knew my brothers and sister were probably mortified that some kids would see them and our circus. No one could really see me in the camper and I was glad.

To the right of this intersection and one block down was our new house. My parents came to Lanesboro several months before and purchased it. I had no idea what it looked like, only that mother said it was very big. Five bedrooms, a twenty two foot long living room, a dining room, a library, several bathrooms, a root cellar, many huge walk in closets, a wrap-around porch and a double stalled barn up in the back of the yard for horses. Soon after we moved in, father built a corral and bought a Shetland pony for my sister and a Saddlebred that my mother had picked out. He also built several floor to ceiling monkey cages. There was a bonus room in the back of the house and half of it became Sally's floor to ceiling cage. We would open the window and she could go outside on the back porch where she had an adjoining eleven by seven foot cage to enjoy the outdoors, and all the neighborhood kids who came to see her. He strung big ropes throughout the cages for Sally to swing on and she would put on a show for them. Silly Sally was her nickname and was bestowed upon her by my new friend Laura. She liked Sally. If I had a quarter for every kid that came into my yard after school to see Sally swing on her ropes I would have been rich! And when she rattled her cage the whole neighborhood heard it. I don't think Doc Westbrook liked it too much though. He was the retired town doctor and lived across the back ally from us. Sometimes when I would be walking home from grade school I would see him standing in his back yard looking over at Sally. His hands would be on his hips and he would be shaking his head back and forth in discontent. I don't think Doc Westbrook liked our monkeys.

Father took a right at the intersection and drove down Main Street to Sylvan Park where he turned the camper around and headed back up Main Street past the small library, then a small white building that was a community center and parked in front of our new house, which was on Main Street. I saw my brothers and sister jump out of the car with two of our dogs (Trixie and Oscar) on leashes. They quickly ventured up the stone steps and went inside the house to explore. Then I saw my father get out of the car, stretch his back and adjust his pants. I was waiting impatiently for mother to come and help me. I had Sally on her leash and two more dogs on leashes (Bambie and LuLubell). She walked down the side of the camper and as soon as the dogs heard her grab the handle, all havoc broke loose. The animals were restless and turning inside out with excitement. This was making Sally a little upset and she started acting up, trying to break free from my grip. I didn't get a chance to clean up the grape jelly covered with coffee grounds and meal worms yet and unfortunately, the refrigerator was opposite the door. The dogs were jumping and covering themselves with this gooey, purple, sticky mess with meal worms swimming in it. As the excitement grew from moment to moment and as I was trying to warn my mother not to open the door until I had a firm grip on the dog's leashes, Sally broke free from my grasp and ran to the door right through the purple mess along with the dogs and waited for it to open. I knew this wouldn't be good. I saw the handle wiggle and again hollered for my mother not to open the door yet. "Wait mom" I hollered but she couldn't hear me. All of the commotion, the barking and my yelling was really upsetting Sally. She jumped up onto the handle, opened the door and bolted out right past my mother. Sally was gone. It all happened so fast, up to the point where I was standing face to face with my mother. Then things happened in slow motion, almost to a point of no motion. Trauma does that to a kid. Then there was the look of bewilderment on mother's face; the jaw drop, the furrowed eyebrows and worst of all the pursed lips, It was an image that I will take to my grave. Then she screamed and set things back in motion. "What in the world happened Melody? "For God's sake go and catch that monkey!"

I didn't say a word and jumped out of the camper chasing after Sally. My mother said she went running towards Sylvan Park where we had just turned our load around a bit ago. There were lots of big trees and I imagined Sally was going to climb up one of them, screaming in her new and unfamiliar terrain. I had her in my sight but she was moving fast running down the sidewalk on her two hind feet, arms outstretched and tail flailing back and forth. Her diaper was starting to fall off too which made for a funny sight. I almost caught up with her and I almost stopped the dragging leash with my foot when she took a sharp turn into the park and up the first tree she saw. By the time I reached her, poor Sally was petrified. I had never seen her so wild eyed. I coaxed her down with open arms and lucky for me she reluctantly descended. She was sticky and purple from the spilled grape jelly but I didn't see any meal worms stuck in her fur thank goodness. I couldn't touch those wiggly things. I managed to carry Sally home without further incidence. As I looked around I realized how pretty this little town was. There was a big river across from Sylvan Park and a beautiful water fall feeding it. Bluffs surrounded the town and there was grass everywhere. The sounds of chirping birds replaced the constant hum of traffic that I was used to in New York. I really liked the old railroad tracks and the old railroad bridge.

As it turned out that was going to become one of many hang out spots for the teens and was right across the street from my house.

When I reached the car I walked right back into the chaos. My older brother Danny was carrying suitcases up the steps into the house and my older brother David and sister Tammy were tying the barking dogs up to any tree they could find in the yard. My mother was standing on the sidewalk holding Shawn, supervising and directing. Across the street and down a block was Hanson's Filling Station. There were at least three or four kids gathered there drinking pop and watching us. There were also several old folks standing in a circle rubber necking. I didn't see my father though and I figured he was in the house. That was okay with me because his big personality would have brought more attention to us and that was not okay with me. Between the four dogs barking, rounding up the cats, Shawn in his bright blue sweater and me chasing after a runaway Spider monkey, that was enough for one day. That was the first day.

GETTING TO KNOW YOU

The dust settled after a week or so and my family and I were enjoying exploring the big house and barn. My father was busy setting up his antique shops, building monkey cages, horse corrals and buying up the town. He bought one of the biggest houses in Lanesboro, two buildings on Main Street and a cute little house a few blocks up the street for my oldest sister and her family. The town folk referred to that part of town as "Brooklyn". It was literally only four blocks away so I thought it unusual to have its own name. Fitting though don't you think? (after all, my father was from the Bronx, New York which isn't too far from Brooklyn, New York). There was also a part of town called Little Norway which was across the river about two football fields away from the old railroad bridge. Then there were the Flats on the north end of town and The Oxtrail which was right above Little Norway. Soon I would learn all about these separate parts of Lanesboro and the significance they held. The town was a historical site and it had over 100 years of rich history and wonderful stories. My house was built in the mid 1800's and used to be where the local newspaper was printed, The Lanesboro Leader. There was a very large area that had its own entrance on the street level and that was where the newspaper was printed. It would also become one of my father's antique shops, then my mother's shop, then my mother's day care center and finally in 1982, my first studio apartment.

I think it's fair to say that when you take a big New York family and move them to a small farm town, they will become celebrities or freaks. I don't think we were celebrities except for my step-dad. I didn't pay too much attention to his affairs but I'm guessing he was a celebrity, with his big personality and his big wallet. The kids around the neighborhood were friendly and curious. They weren't shy about hanging around the house and introducing themselves. Most of them really liked our monkeys. Remember when I said what a few of my favorite things were…my clothes, my friends and cute boys? Well I was getting plenty of attention from the boys and several girls were willing to befriend my sister and me pretty quick. That was good. My clothes and my accent were the hurdle. The fashion I left behind was Mary Jane flats and knee high socks, pleated skirts and coordinating tops. Like I said, I loved my clothes as all thirteen year old girls do. I noticed that most everyone here was dressed in a relaxed, country denim style and there was nothing wrong with that except for the fact that I didn't own a pair of denim jeans. It was polyester for me. Many of the girls wore denim bib overalls, blue Nike tennis shoes and jean jackets with a zip-up hoodie under it. I didn't see anyone wearing knee high socks, Mary Jane flats or pleated skirts and it was apparent that I had to change my style of clothes to fit in. My mother took us shopping at the Apache Mall in Rochester where she grew up. My grandmother was a retired head nurse on the gastroenterology ward at the Mayo Clinic and my mother graduated from Lourdes Catholic High School. Her ties to Minnesota were what brought us back here. My grandparents, who lived just outside of Rochester, were getting old and we wanted to be closer to them.

Blue Nike tennis shoes took the place of my cute Mary Janes. Denim jeans and bib overalls were my new style. I threw out my flowered polyester pants and coordinating top. They were simply unacceptable if I wanted to fit in. To be honest with you, I could run faster in the Nikes and I was beginning to like my new look. I felt like a tom boy and a new me started to evolve. It didn't take long to fall in love with the horses and I rode them every chance I could get. My mother subscribed to popular horse magazines. She tutored me to ride western and English style. Soon I would make several more friends in my new home town who were riders. Goodbye Mary Janes and hello cowboy boots. The bibs really completed the picture as I shoveled the manure out of the horse stalls. I didn't realize how smelly manure could be and it was a very unpleasant job for this New York kid. Sometimes the barn smell would emanate throughout the neighborhood and I don't think the town folks liked that. We had one Shetland pony named Jack. Then my father bought my mother a beautiful Saddlebred who we called Mariah. Soon to follow was our Quarter horse Sunbeam and then Rufus, a POA (Pony of America). On a warm summer's day the barn smell would get pretty strong. The town authorities told my folks that we could only have one or two horses at the most because we were in the city limits. When my mother told me this we chuckled a bit together because we felt Lanesboro was not a city at all, not like what we were used to. My new friends Lorie, Marcia and Kate (they were sisters) also owned a Shetland pony and they told us where they pastured him on the edge of town. My father contacted a Mr. Drake and soon our horses were out to pasture as well. We kept one or two at the most at home in the corral and I soon learned what the word "chore" really meant. Each morning I would have to get out of bed early before school and walk up our very hilly back yard to feed and water the horses. As soon as I opened the back kitchen door, they would let out a very loud whinny in anticipation for their food. Instead of a rooster to wake up the neighbors, it was the sound of several horses and was much prettier. My step-dad should have been born a Texan, because he went big on everything. It was difficult to keep a low profile in such a small town. He didn't think he was causing attention, but his big spending was giving us a reputation of being wealthy and aloof with money. One or two horses would have been enough. Soon to add to our small herd would be Charlie, a fifteen hand high thoroughbred and Morningstar, who was fourteen hands high and had a white star on her forehead. I loved all of our horses though and soon I would learn how to groom, halter, bridle and saddle a horse as well as become a pretty good rider, but I never got used to that smell on a warm summer's day. Sometimes when I would be in the corral grooming a horse, I would see Doc Westbrook looking over at our place in discontent. His hands would be on his hips and his head would be shaking in a disapproving sort of way. I don't think the old doctor liked our horses too much.

MORNINGSTAR'S STORY

The winters in Port Jefferson were cold and snowy but not like in Minnesota. Back home we used sleds instead of inner tubes or plastic sliding saucers. I liked the sleds better because you could steer them away from trees or other kids. A popular spot to slide in Lanesboro was my back yard and ally. If I was cold I could duck inside for a quick warm up and a cup of hot coco. In fact, almost all the houses around the ally had kids my age. There was Lisa (I found out later that her dad was a beloved town cop along with old Cody), Nancy, Lorie and little Brenda, who was as cute as a button. Then there was Chad, Jeff, Pat, Tom and little Lesa, who was also as cute as a button. Next to the old doc's house lived Steve, Tim, Samantha and Jason. Some of the kids were not happy after my dad built the corral for the horses because it blocked the sliding path from the top of the steep alley and down to my yard where the terraces created moguls that intensified the fun.

Sometimes the older boys would keep a look-out for traffic and if the coast was clear and it always was, they would slide right off the last terrace, over the stone wall and onto the sidewalk of Main Street. I remember little Jason who was a cute kid with blond wavy hair. He went sliding down the hill too fast and lost control. Jason hit a tree so hard that I thought I heard his head crack. His siblings rushed him home that day and I guess his injury wasn't that serious, not that I heard anyway.

After the corral was built the kids had to re-route the sliding hill or steep ally. The ride was shorter but safer because there weren't any trees to run into. The first few Minnesota winters took some getting used to. Our normal winter gear wasn't enough to ward off the cold and we had to learn how to really bundle up. That meant double or triple socks, long johns under our snow pants instead of tights, thick water proof mittens over gloves, snowmobile boots if you wanted to outlast everyone, a thick face mask and then a hood tied into place with a scarf that covered your mouth and nose over the face mask. Minnesota kids are hardy and can endure very cold days, sliding for hours at a time. We also learned as a family that we had to check on the horses more often during a cold snap. This one particular season was exceptionally cold with the temperatures dropping well below zero for days on end. We usually had two horses at home at one time. They would be in the corral during the day and the barn at night. We didn't have a horse trailer so we would have to walk them about 1.5 miles to Drake's pasture and rotate them often from home. The barn worked great for keeping our beloved horses out of the bitter cold. We could have put more than a couple in the barn for shelter during that winter, but the city rules stated no more than one or two at a time. Mother was concerned for our horses in the pasture on this particularly cold day and she asked my sister and me to go and check on them. The walk was up the alley, past the Lutheran church, the elementary school, the Catholic Church and on the very end of the street. We were bundled up real good so the walk wasn't too bad. When we reached the pasture we called for the horses. Sunbeam and Rufus were home in the barn and Charlie, Captain and Morningstar were at Drakes. A trick we used to get the horses to come was to shake a bag of horse chow while we called them, just like shaking a bag of cat food to get cats to come. There was a shelter on the east side of the pasture and we waited there for the horses while calling them and shaking the bag of food. This was their first winter in the pasture and I don't think they were too familiar with their surroundings. I didn't know how big the area was but many times it would be ten or fifteen minutes before the horses would show up, but this time we only saw Charlie and Captain. It was really cold and windy. I wondered why all three horses weren't hunkered down in the shelter for protection. They were smart so I figured it was because they didn't know their way around the pasture yet. I noticed in the snow that there were no fresh hoof prints, and that meant they were out there for one night and an entire day during the fresh snow fall and windy frigid temperatures. I started to get worried when Morningstar didn't show up. I thought maybe her hoofs were cold and she was moving slower than the other two. So my sister and I ventured down the same path where Captain and Charlie came up and we found her. There she was lying on her side, motionless and a bit bloated. A light dusting of snow covered her body and some more snow drifted up against her belly from the wind. Our poor Morningstar was dead. It was an awful sight and the vision is as clear in my mind now as it was the day we found her. I remember feeling sick to my stomach when I saw her from a combination of grotesqueness and sadness, mostly sadness. When I think back now I believe she probably died from exposure.I think she got lost and couldn't find her way back to the shelter, but it was strange to me that the other two horses survived and she didn't. My sister and I knew we needed to get home as soon as possible and tell mother what had happened. We ran home as fast as our young bundled up bodies could go, it was a silent and solemn trip back, poor Morningstar.

GOING DOWN WITH MARIAH

Main Street was about one mile long from the north end of town where it touched the root river and continued straight up to the golf course where it ended, which only added insult to injury as that road had its own steep hill. I know this because sometimes our track coach, Mrs. Post would have us run this route. Many grueling practices entailed running up and down the grade from the football field and back, which incidentally helped produce a Lanesboro hero who was such a fast runner that she made it to the pre-Olympic try outs. She was kind enough to let me run with her, but it was only once because my fastest pace was her slowest pace. I respected her a great deal and admired her running ability, which encouraged me to get my two mile run down to a little over twelve minutes which helped me to sail through basic training in my later years. The town had a wonderful parade for her when she returned from the try-outs. Her name was Lorie. Her brother was a fast runner too and his nick name was Bullet. Karen was a good runner as well and she didn't mind the grade. She lived a few miles from the top and sometimes I would see her walking home before she got her first car. For a new comer, the grade appeared long and steep but not for the local kids who were used to it. If I wasn't in track then I was on the bleachers cheering on the burros. It was always exciting watching Lorie run so fast, but even more fun seeing the looks on the spectator's faces from other competing towns as she jetted around the track. Lorie was a part of Lanesboro's pride and she earned her own legacy.

Mariah was our sixteen hand high Saddlebred. She was chestnut colored and gorgeous. Mariah had a mild personality and a strong body. She loved to run and It was fun getting her into a fast canter or gallop whenever I could. The saying is true about Saddlebreds, and that is "it feels like you are riding on air". She had the smoothest canter I had ever experienced. Even her trot was fluid. Oh the excitement I would feel when running a big Saddlebred like Mariah. That horse and I had a bond. I took care of her and she took care of me. It was always a challenge when I had to saddle Mariah because she was so tall and I was short. Mother kept a stool in the barn so I could stand on it to reach her back while I hoisted up the heavy western saddle. She was trained well and stood still for me. Mariah didn't even fuss when I tightened up the cinch, unlike Charlie who would blow up his stomach before cinching. All of you equestrians out there know what this means…that after the horse relaxes the cinch would eventually loosen and the saddle would slip down one side or the other. Some horses just didn't like getting saddled and would do this on purpose. I usually rode Charlie bareback to avoid a battle of the wills and get him mad at me. Charlie had a biting problem too. He was sort of a naughty horse. Mariah on the other hand, loved to go for rides. My usual route was to take her up the ally, past the Lutheran Church, then the Catholic Church and turn right at the elementary school on top of the hill. Then I would hit my first stretch and away we would go. She knew what I wanted and she wanted it too. It wouldn't be long before we were in a full canter, almost a fast gallop. Then at the end of the road I would slow her down to a trot, take another right and pass my older sister's house which was up Brooklyn (I know it sounds funny to say it that way but that's how everyone said it). My little nephew Sammy would be out playing in his yard almost all the time and he loved to see his aunt Melody come riding by. Mariah knew my route and our destination. I could feel her anticipation as she would tug on the reigns to hurry and get there, to our "racing gate". She was such a smart horse and I swear she could read my mind.

At the base of the golf course there was a long stretch of road that was flat and a perfect place to giddy up a horse, which I always did. Before Mariah and I took off, I vaguely remember mother telling me not to run her on the pavement because she didn't have horse shoes on at the time and it wouldn't be good for her hoofs. What I do remember was the run. We started at the beginning of the road where the intersection was and our intentions were to trot, canter, gallop and then run in that order, until we reached the end of the road which was at the Olson's house where Jeff, Jennifer, Becky, Craig and their beautiful black lab lived. We were at the starting point and Mariah pulled at the bit. She was ready to go. I settled deep in the saddle and made sure I had a good grip on the reigns. I positioned my feet in the stirrups with heals down and toes up, just like mother taught me. Then I leaned forward and whispered in her left ear, "Ready to go girl?" She was. I tucked forward a little more, squeezed my knees and yelled "giddy-up". Mariah took off as if she was at a race track waiting for the gate to open and I was the jockey. We hit our trot and quickly went into a smooth canter, then gallop and ultimately a fast, smooth run! I was in heaven. Now that I think about it that could have been a great possibility after what happened next.

We passed the first three blocks, then ran onward and passed the first two intersections. When we reached the base of the hill on the left that led up to the golf course everything went terribly wrong. All at once Mariah shied from something she saw on the road, tried to jute to the left, slipped on the pavement and we wiped out. We hit the ground hard and she landed on my foot and ankle while it was twisted in a weird and contorted way from the stirrup. Mariah recovered before me and was back up on her feet within seconds. My immediate concern was the possibility of my horse breaking a leg. As for me, I was all scratched up from road rash and my ankle looked like it was broken. I didn't know how I was going to get Mariah home, or how I was going to get back up in that saddle. I was in a lot of pain and I couldn't stand up on my foot. Then an angel came by on his bike; a young angel with curly hair and thick glasses. His name was Duane, but we called him Henry.

I saw him racing toward us on his bike and he looked more panicked than me. He came to a quick stop by my side and asked me if I was ok. I said I was fine but my horse was getting away. I asked him to go catch her by the reigns but not to run up to her, to approach her slowly saying her name over and over. He was a brave little kid considering Mariah was so big. He didn't have horses and wasn't used to them. But on this day Henry was a little horseman. He caught Mariah and led her back to me. Then Henry helped me to get up and into the saddle, which was still in place because Mariah didn't blow up her stomach when I tightened the cinch. Little Duane was my hero. He was a short stocky kid and his nick name was Henry Kissinger because, well he looked just like Henry Kissinger. After my horse and I regained our senses, I thanked Henry for helping me and went on my way. As I turned to wave goodbye, I saw him jump off his bike and run into his house, no doubt to tell his mom what had just happened and that he was a hero that day.

I let Mariah do most of the leading home and we went the quickest way, which was straight down main street. When we reached my house mother and grandmother were sitting on the porch swing and they both saw us coming from blocks away. At this point I didn't have much control over the horse. I was injured and in pain. After my mother called out my name and said those old familiar words I've heard more often than I cared to, "Melody what happened?" "You ran Mariah didn't you". Before I could utter out a guilty affirmative answer, the horse reacted to her voice and took total control of the reins. There were thirteen stone steps to the first landing, then another six steps to the porch. Mariah surprised us all when she took it upon herself to climb those two set of stairs and up the hilly back yard to her corral. This time it wasn't my mom who assumed the classical look of bewilderment, but my grandmother. The jaw drop, the furrowed eyebrows and worse than anything else, the pursed lips. That look must be hereditary. Mom and grandma hurried up to the barn and helped me unsaddle Mariah and take the bit out of her mouth. She didn't get her routine brush down that day as I usually enjoyed our quiet time together after a ride. That's when we bonded. Instead I was lying in my bed with my foot elevated on some pillows, ace wrapped and iced, and a few extra-large band aids on my elbows and hip from the road rash. With my grandmother being a retired nurse there was no avoiding the treatment. Lucky for me it was only a bad sprain and even more so, my beautiful horse was ok. I still wonder to this day what Mariah shied from. There were no puddles or anything like that. Maybe she saw a little snake.

SNAKES, SNAKES, SNAKES!

Two years had passed since the first day and the year was 1976. My family was adjusting well, but slowly. Our accents had to go and we were working on that. Most of the people living in Lanesboro were Norwegian descendants and they spoke with a strong accent. My family and I had to learn many new and harmless expletives like uffda and don't ya know. I met a very nice riding partner named Lolly and she had a pretty Quarter horse named Flicka. She and I would sometimes take our horses out together and she would give me advice on how to ride, how to talk and fit in. Lolly was a few years older and she kind of took me in as a little sister. Honestly I think she felt sorry for me because the teasing was relentless. Lolly also warned me about the many snakes that we would encounter and to keep watch for them when we were riding outside of town and in the ditches. She said that many years ago Lanesboro was infested with rattlesnakes and they were still a bit of a problem, more of a nusance than a danger. I found out quickly that this was true as I often saw rattlesnakes sunning near the dam. Sometimes I would see them lying under the railroad tracks across from my house. Lolly mentioned something about two brothers that were from Lanesboro, and quite a few years ago she said they were hired by the town to clear out over a thousand rattle snakes. Their names were Johnny and Arnie Rank.

The Newgarden's lived across the ally from my house and the kids and I became friends. Lesa told me more about the Ranks. She said the brother's used to skin the rattlers in the ally and they used to call the kids "little chipmunks" when they would gather around to watch. It made me nervous to imagine so many rattle snakes once inhabited this little town. I would be extra cautious when pulling out a hay bale from the barn to feed the horses. My new friends told me that rattle snakes liked barns and hay piles, so I was sure to be alert. Thank goodness the snakes couldn't climb up to the hay loft because that quickly became a neighborhood hangout, without mother knowing of course. Thoen's Hotel was parallel to my house. In fact the buildings were so close that there were only a few feet in between. A small shaggy hedge separated our back yard from the hotel's back yard and Doc Westbrook's house was right across the alley from the hotel, which appeared to be abandoned except for a little room that could be accessed from the back entrance and was right across from my kitchen window. It was a big old hotel and was built in the 1800's.

The front faced Main Street as my house did and to drive by them was like something out of an old western. The train across from my house was still running through town at that time. It was a steam engine and would pass through Lanesboro often, which added to the old western ambiance. The train and tracks were gutted out in the late 70's and replaced with miles and miles of bike trails. Thoen's Hotel was a ghost hotel when we moved to Lanesboro. It was deserted, dark and spooky. At night while I was washing the supper dishes I would often see a very old man in one of the back rooms sitting by the window. It was the only room that was lit up and the curtain was always open. There wasn't much activity in that room day or night, just this little old man that would sit in his chair, night after night chain smoking. It was Johnny Rank. Many evenings the neighborhood kids would meet and sit on the front steps of the hotel and many times I would join them. I didn't realize that the little old man who came and went from the back entrance was Johnny Rank. He would venture out of the hotel and head uptown to buy his cigarettes. A carton of camel straights no filter is what he always had in his hand. He was one of the lucky smokers who baffled the medical profession and beat the odds because he lived to be quite old. Johnny walked very slow, more of a shuffle and was a bit hunched over. He always wore faded bib overalls and always had a cap on. I wondered how good his hearing was. I was concerned that he would be annoyed when Sally shook her cage because his room was about fifty feet away from it. His beard was long and grey with tobacco stains around his mouth and mustache. He was a pleasant old man and I could see it in his eyes as he would always say hi to us youngsters. I was told that his brother Arnie Rank died some years earlier and that the two were always together. They worked as a team to clear out approximately 2,000 Timber Rattlesnakes that were infesting Lanesboro and the surrounding farms. Johnny and Arnie were Lanesboro's heroes and earned their impressive reputations from days gone past. Johnny would slowly shuffle along walking the streets of Lanesboro alone, carrying with him a legacy that should never be forgotten. I am amazed that those two fellas could catch so many rattle snakes without a lethal bite, again beating the odds. This was one of my favorite stories. The Rank brothers didn't get all the rattlesnakes though. I'm sure they had to leave some of them alone so the elements of nature could continue. There were plenty of snakes left in Lanesboro that weren't venomous and I still kept a watchful eye when I was walking the Oxtrail or riding horses in the ditch. The Root River flowed through the edge town and coupled with the surrounding bluffs, made for a perfect breeding ground for snakes, especially bull snakes.

THE OLD BRIDGE

Lanesboro had many hang outs where the kids would…hang out. Personally I liked the railroad bridge because I only had to cross the street to go home at curfew, but the old bridge had its advantages as well. First of all it was situated right next to the ball park which made for an exciting night when there was a game. The ball park was situated right at the base of the grade. The same grade that took the life of a semi-truck driver years ago, and the same grade that scared Sally and I half to death.

There was a rope that someone had tied to the belly of the old bridge and my new friends and I would have many fun times swinging out over the river and jumping in. It was a great swimming spot and the current was tame there, but there was still a current. The swimming hole was about twelve feet deep and many brave young men would jump off the bridge and into the water. This was a popular "sport" in Lanesboro, but risky. Young thrill seekers had to make sure their target was accurate, because right before the swimming hole was shallow rapids which were only about ankle deep. It was a great spot for the river rats to cross. Some were small and some were pretty large. The sun didn't shine too much over the old bridge and it was cool and shaded underneath, and usually a little muddy. This "down town" area of Lanesboro was populated with a couple of small diners, taverns and the feed mill. It was a smorgasbord for rodents who made a comfortable home under the cool bridge to bear their fatted off-spring. Many times I would see a river rat or two running along under the bridge but for the most part, they stayed clear. Some of them were pretty big, but not too much for the bull snakes to handle and there were plenty of bull snakes that lived under the old bridge. These snakes were non-venomous and could grow as big as six feet long and two inches thick. There was one den in particular that I will never forget which was under the left side of the bridge. We would inevitably disturb that big old snake and more often than I cared to, I witnessed his fast and slithering retreat into his den. As long as we didn't disturb him, he didn't disturb us. That was our agreement.

It was a very warm day in August of 1978. The closest public swimming pool was in Preston and if we didn't catch the big yellow school bus for a ride there, then it was inner tubing down the root river. This was also a very popular way to cool off and many of my friends were proud of their resilient tubes that could handle the river's rapids and rocks without popping. Canoeing was popular too and I preferred this over the inner tubes because of the river snakes. I didn't like the river snakes and there were many of them. We knew when we would pass a den on the riverbank because there would be many little snakes that would swim together to a certain spot, no doubt alarming mama and papa snake of our intrusion. They didn't seem to swim in the middle of the river where the current was the strongest, but along the banks where the branches of trees leaned out and grew over the river. I also learned that these were good spots to catch rainbow trout as I became an avid fisherman along with everything else. The most important thing I learned was to respect the snakes. Like I said, we didn't disturb them and they didn't disturb us, but occasionally an encounter would arise.

Katie and I missed the bus that warm day in August and decided to hang out under the old bridge and swim. Her big brother Greg had the best inner tubes in town and he was usually pretty generous in sharing. Katie and I agreed to meet at the old bridge after going home and changing out of our swimming suits to get into some cut-offs, t-shirts and old tennis shoes (the river was no place for a young girl barefoot and in a bikini). By the time I got to the bridge I had worked up a sweat and was anxious to jump in. Katie was already there waiting for me with a big black tube she had borrowed from Greg. She reminded me to clear the dirt path of any resting snakes first by banging a stick on the ground and in the bushes, a quick tutorial from a country girl to a city slicker. The coast was clear so we continued on the path and down under the bridge. The cool shade felt good. I was glad to see a vacancy from the big old bull snake, who had a den on the other side. I thought he was probably inside escaping from the heat and I was glad. He was big, ugly and fast but never bothered us. After I was sure that the coast was clear I called Katie down the little dirt trail and we didn't hesitate to jump in with the tube. The cool water felt great, there were no river rats about and big old Mr. Bull snake was tucked away in his den. Things couldn't have been better. Katie and I dunked our heads a few times then climbed on up on the inner tube. I was on one side and she was on the other and our feet were in the middle knee deep in water. As we were kicking to maintain our spot against the mild current, I hit something and thought it was Katie's foot. Then things happened in slow motion, almost to a point of no motion. Just like the time when Sally busted loose from the camper and took off running down the sidewalk on her hind feet with her diaper falling off, arms wailing back and forth and tail flailing. That was a funny site, but our encounter with the snake was not. Big old Mr. Bull snake was not in his den. He was in the river, in the swimming hole with us!

I apologized to Katie for kicking her foot and hoped it didn't hurt her. She looked at me in a funny sort of way and said, "You didn't kick my foot". I quickly looked down into the water and lifted my leg only to see the tail end of a very big snake swim over my foot. I hollered "snake" and this is when things were back in motion. We bailed, screaming in a state of panic and fought the current to reach the muddy river bank as fast as we could to get out of the water. I imagine we were quite a sight to see. I wasn't too concerned about the inner tube and neither was Katie. Our will to survive took precedence and the tube was flowing down the root river and on its way to Whalen. We contemplated interceding the empty tube by beating it to the next set of shallow rapids which was three quarters of a mile away under the highway 250 bridge (there were a lot of bridges in Lanesboro) but it was a feeble attempt. We couldn't compete with the rivers current and took our loss. The root river flowed past the small towns of Whalen, Peterson and then Rushford which was always our destination when tubing in a big group of kids. It would take all day and someone would always be there to give us a ride back to Lanesboro. Katie's brother Greg wasn't happy when we told him that we had lost his inner tube. He had more but we never dared ask him again if we could use one. I didn't partake in any more river excursions for the rest of that summer and I stayed clear from the old bridge. My new hang out was the railroad bridge which was conveniently right across the street from my house.

ITCHY AND THE RAILROAD BRIDGE

It was September, chilly and rainy but not cold enough to hang out under the new bridge where we could be protected from the wind. I had only been under there a few times because that was where the older kids would hang out. Besides, I liked the rail road bridge the most because we could actually sit on the wooden walk way which was level with the bridge instead of sitting underneath it, and I could see my front porch. There were mature trees around hiding us from view, but close enough to the street light for us to see. There weren't any snake dens around as far as I knew. But if we were to walk the trail along the railroad tracks up to the dam, we would most likely run into one. Right above the waterfall was a popular party spot and the only way to get to it would be to climb up an eight foot rocky stepped cliff, just off the tracks. The kids had chairs and a fire pit up there. The river was about twenty feet away on one side and there was about a fifteen foot drop onto the tracks below on the other side. It was a pretty spot but very dark and a bit remote. There were too many snakes around the dam and I was happy we stayed at the old railroad bridge that night.

If it wasn't for the muddy banks of the Root River Itchy would have certainly broken his ankle or leg I'm sure. Itchy was a dare devil and in retrospect, I think he knew the muddy bank would cushion his impact, that's why he jumped. I was fifteen years old and he was sixteen. No kid would pull such a crazy stunt unless they were stupid or trying to impress a girl, I guess. Lanesboro was a very sleepy town and there wasn't much for a young person to do unless they were farmers. I knew kids who were dairy farmers, pig farmers, turkey farmers, beef farmers and crop farmers. I rarely saw them outside of school because their work was never done. Those were the kids that would most often get wild at a party after a Friday night game. I guess because they were cooped up all week out in the country. But in town it could be boring too. There wasn't a bowling alley or a recreation center. No girl scouts or dance lessons and 4-H was mostly the farm kids showing their horses, prize pigs, or prize cows and such. My circle of friends was diverse. I didn't just hang out with the city kids but spent many a day on the McCabe farm or the Flattum place which were several miles out in the country. They were isolated but could be a lot of fun. Some of my memories include taking an old pick-up truck down the gravel road and back with my friend Patty. Neither of us had our driver's licenses and I didn't know how to drive yet. Neither did she too well because we ended up in the pig pen coming down the driveway on the way back. I learned quickly not to call the pig pen the pig coup or the chicken coup the chicken pen, and the difference between a combine and a hay bailer, and that John Deere was the best manufacturer for tractors. I enjoyed being on a farm but could never get used to picking out a chicken from the coup, watching it be butchered and then help pluck it in preparation for the evening meal. I guess if you do it all the time there's nothing to it and the meat is fresh and healthy. I certainly didn't experience anything like that in New York.

I wasn't thirteen anymore and started to take an interest in other forms of entertainment besides inner tubing or swinging on ropes tied under bridges, and that would have been boys, pot and beer. After all, this was the 70's and weed was very popular and common. It was growing wild all around the outside of town. Itchy called it "home grown". Sometimes there would be stronger weed in circulation that someone had brought in from LaCrosse or Rochester and it was much better than home grown. I was an avid runner and wasn't a pot head by any means. Lanesboro was no drug town and the pot was usually pretty mellow and harmless. My family and I left the drugs and gangs in New York. I saw Mike and Itchy hanging out at the railroad bridge across the street and they saw me sitting on my porch. It wasn't dark out yet and I still had several hours until curfew, which was right after dark. Mike and Itchy were friends of my brothers and my mother knew them by him. She thought they were nice boys and didn't mind if I went to hang out with them as long as I was home by curfew. I didn't mind because they were boys. I enjoyed hanging out with the guys as much as the girls. After a short while we got bored and decided to walk uptown and find someone who had some weed. We were also hoping to find a kind soul who would buy us some beer. The fun was just beginning.

It was going to be dark soon and we still couldn't find someone to buy us beer. It had to be Schmidt beer. I thought it tasted pretty good and at that age I was content with just one can, so a six pack was really all we wanted. There were several taverns in Lanesboro and our strategy would be to linger outside the bar until a kid who was of age would come out. Then we would ask and they would usually say yes. After all, the same was done for them when they were young and the tradition carried on. Mostly, they went through the same small town boredom when they were kids and understood our motivation. We first stopped at Rose's tavern and looked in the window, but there was no one inside for us. We then checked the liquor store, the tavern across the street called "The Excuse" and the American Legion but still no luck. Our last hope was the tavern called "The Bent Elbow" and we hit the jackpot. Mike flagged down Dan from the outside window. Dan knew what we wanted; to meet him in the alley behind the tavern for beer. Our hit was a success and we gave him five bucks for the six pack of Schmidt. It was easy smuggling the beer to the railroad bridge because the town was pretty dead and there was really no one to catch us. There was Cody, the town cop who would cruise up and down Main Street real slow, but he usually spent most of his probable boring and uneventful shifts idling at Sylvan Park. Sometimes hours would go by until a car would slowly cruise down main street. When we got to the bridge there was still an hour of daylight left. We settled in where we couldn't be seen from the street and cracked open a beer. I really didn't like to drink but choked one down to fit in. The boys drank a lot more than me and soon the beer had almost run out. We were laughing and having a good time until the boys decided to play dare devil and climb up to the top of the frame supporting the bridge. I stayed where I was which was already about thirty feet from the river bank below, but from the top where the boys were sitting on the twelve inch beam, that added another twenty feet. The top of the bridge, I surmised was roughly fifty five feet from the muddy river bank below. They coaxed me to climb up but I wouldn't have done that for a hundred bucks. Mike and Itchy sat up there together until Itchy finished the last beer. It was nearly dark and I asked them to come down. Mike did, but Itchy wasn't satisfied with his stunt. He asked us to make a target down on the river bank, he said he wanted to hit it with his empty beer can. So Mike and I ventured down to the grassy trail and piled up several rocks for him to hit, which he did with accuracy. Then Itchy did the unthinkable. He stood up on that twelve inch beam and said he was going to jump. Mike shouted in a loud whisper, "No Itchy, it's too high. Come on down and don't be dumb". I thought, If he jumps he's going to die. This kid with the goofy nick-name is going to die and at that moment he was air born. Lucky for him it had been heavily raining the past few days. Lucky for him he missed the target and landed in the muddy river bank. It was a loud thump and I thought the worst. Mike and I ran to him and by the grace of God Itchy was okay. No obvious broken bones or injuries. The only problem Mike and I had was pulling him out of the mud as he was a little more than ankle deep in it.

The old rail road bridge continues to stand strong and is now a gateway to the state bike trail that passes Little Norway, and the ever so beautiful water fall. I imagine the town kids still gather together there for pow-wows and that people fish from the bank just like we used to. Itchy never did recover his old convers on that chilly September night. Who knows, maybe the sneakers are still there, deep in the mud two feet under.

THE WHITMORE BROTHERS

I wondered for a long time why everyone called that kid Itchy. I didn't ask because I was learning that there were many other people with funny nick names too. For instance, Caveman, Speed, Animal, Bullet, Zeek or Little Tuna (he had two), and Quail just to name a few. Those were nick names for the guys. There weren't so many for the girls but the ones that stand out in my memory were Purple Turd, Laura Lie, LB and Schmell, which was bestowed upon me by my friend Laura. There was no need to grow a thick skin because I learned quickly that these were names of endearment and were not meant to be malicious or mean in any way. Just about everyone had a nick name but it's difficult to recall all of them and some were very imaginative. Most had a meaning or story behind them. I thought Itchy got his nick name because of his curly hair and I thought he was cute, but after his crazy and death defying stunt I wiped him off my list for potential boyfriends. It wasn't until several years later that he told me why his name was Itchy and it made perfect sense. It seemed that he was a dare devil many years ago, not just that chilly night in September. It was because of the fire.

Several years before I moved to Lanesboro around 1970 Itchy told me that he, his cousin and the Whitmore brothers were hanging out in some old barn off country road 250. It was summer vacation and I guess there wasn't much for them to do. The boys were bored and decided to go exploring so they rode their bikes for several miles out of town. They came across an abandoned building, I think he said it was a barn and managed to get into mischief which is what many young boys do. After all "boys will be boys" and that quote has proven over time to mean potential injury or danger.

These four young kids decided to go and have a look and for reasons only known to them, they also decided to play with fire in that old and dried up barn. The boys didn't realize he said that the fire would have spread as fast as it did, trapping them behind a wall of flames. He told me that his cousin (I'll call him Mitch for the sake of privacy) was the unsung hero that day because he pulled the boys out of the fire and saved their lives. Then Mitch raced his bike back to town and got help. One of the brothers was burned very badly and was seriously injured. I remember him well not only because he was one of the first kids I met, but because the disfiguring scars on his face didn't stop his charm from spilling out. He wasn't a bit shy and introduced himself to me. His is eyes sparkled as he reached out his hand to shake mine. I made a point not to look away. Besides, the scars on his face really didn't bother me. In my opinion this Whitmore boy still had plenty of pretty left. I didn't feel sorry for him either and I treated him the same as I treated all of my new friends. He didn't hang out too much and I didn't get to know him real well, but I will never forget him. Itchy showed me the burns on his back and shoulder from the fire. He had pronounced scarring as well. Itchy said that when he was healing, the burns itched like crazy and he commenced to scratching, or itching the healed skin and this is why he got the nick name Itchy.

BIG TED TAKES LANESBORO

It was 1980 and I felt like things were going well. My family and pets were finally fitting in. Our East Coast accents were disappearing and my friends liked our monkeys Shawn and Sally. My sister and I each had boyfriends and school was going well for all of us. We either participated in or attended the Friday night games and we were invited to most parties. It was good living the small town life. At this point I felt like a real Minnesota country girl. Life was normal and routine, until that is Big Ted came to town.

His name was Fred and he was my high styling and very flashy big brother. The family has called him Teddy ever since I can remember. When we moved to Lanesboro five years ago Teddy stayed back because he didn't want to leave his friends, girlfriend and job. That was okay because he was old enough to be on his own. He moved to Manhattan and lived in an apartment on Manhattan Avenue. Teddy always had a lot of friends and he always had pretty girlfriends too. He was good looking and had a winning personality. When Big Ted moved to Lanesboro it was one heck of a culture shock. Not so much for him, but for Lanesboro. Teddy had the typical New York personality, just like my dad and he stood out.

I have said it before and I'll say it again, that I think it is fair to speculate when you take a person from New York and move them to a teeny, tiny farm town they are either going to be a celebrity or a freak. Out of us four kids that invaded Lanesboro in 1974, I was the freak. It took me the longest to adjust because I was the one chasing monkeys and refused to give up my polyester for quite some time and wear denim bib overalls like everyone else. When Teddy came to town he was dressed like a real city slicker and had a strong east coast accent, but he was a celebrity.

When Big Ted walked down the sidewalk you could hear his boots with every step. They were black leather cowboy boots, silver tipped and shiny with a thick heal that hit the sidewalk with purpose, setting his dance-like pace. Rhythm, he walked with rhythm. His pants were brown, leather and expensive. Teddy had a good sense of fashion and his black leather jacket matched his black silver tipped boots. Sometimes he wore his brown leather jacket with his black leather pants. Every move he made was deliberate and could be heard like a new leather saddle. He wore colorful shirts like Hawaiian prints or even pink button downs and he wore them well. Teddy loved his rings and sometimes wore a big jade man ring on his right pinky and another flashy gold one on his left. Necklaces weren't something he didn't bother with. I'm guessing because they would get caught in his hairy chest which was clear to see where his shirt buttoned. His ear was pierced adorning a small gold hoop. Teddy had brown loose curly hair and a full mustache. He was attractive, walked with confidence and the girls in Lanesboro loved him. My friends wanted to date him (he was even invited to the high school prom), my girlfriend's moms flirted with him and the guys wanted to be his buddy. Not because he was a looker, but Big Ted was always the life of any party with his gregarious personality and funny jokes. He had an infectious laugh too. Teddy had many skills, from carpentry work to an experienced chef. He was hired at the Branding Iron in Preston and I also worked there as well. The single waitresses competed for his attention and they all wanted to date him. The married waitresses flirted with him. It was exhausting being his little sister.

Teddy took Lanesboro by storm and he was a celebrity from the word go. Actually I think his huge popularity helped my popularity. Come to think of it, I did have more friends when he lived there. He was colorful and I was proud to be his little sister. Big Ted stayed around for a year or two and then moved back to Manhattan. Everyone hated to see him leave and the waitresses at the Branding Iron really missed him. It would be many years before I would see my big brother again. My time to leave Lanesboro was approaching too and soon mother would have an empty nest. Within the next two years I would venture to Rochester and attend St. Mary's School of Practical Nursing. I worked at St. Mary's Hospital in the Cardiac Intensive Care Unit and Joined the Army Reserves. My first unit was the 205th Support Battalion in Rochester where my MOS (Primary Occupational Specialty) was a 91Bravo/Combat Medic and my secondary MOS was a 91Charlie/Practical Nurse. Basic Training came easy for me because I was an avid runner and I felt very comfortable with guns. I fired expert (36 out of 40) at practice record fire and sharpshooter (34 out of 40) at record fire. I was promoted to sergeant quickly because I could score 300 out of 300 on my physical training tests and also because I was a good shot…thanks to Doug Quaid and Mr. Capon.

CAPONS

The smell of gun powder created a feeling of excitement in my stomach. Remember when you were a kid waiting at the bus stop and sometimes the exhaust would hit your nose before the bus arrived and butterflies would get in your stomach? The smell of gun powder, right after I squeezed the trigger did that to me. I was a good shot and managed to retain that accuracy throughout my ten years as a soldier. I would dazzle my drill sergeants and was envied by many of my comrades because I was one of the first ones to qualify on the firing range, which was one of my favorite places to be. My drill instructors would say to me "Private Hall, where'd you learn to fire like that." I had to give two people credit, Mr. Capon and Doug.

I was only sixteen years old when I started working at the white Front café after school. It was my first real job with real paychecks. I worked there for about two years as a waitress and earned a lot of money. While most girls turning sixteen were buying clothes, make up, jewelry or saving up for their first car, I was saving up for something different; something powerful and dangerous.

I first saw it when I was running an errand for my mother. She sent me downtown to Capon's hardware store on Main Street which was close to the drug store, where an ample supply of jewelry, make up and perfume filled their display cases but they were not calling me. The shot gun was. I saw it every time I checked out at the Hardware store when I was on one of many errands. It was beautiful and prominently displayed in the gun rack behind the cash register. The shot gun was a Stevens 12 gauge single barrel. The butt was made of carved wood and it fit well into my shoulder. Mr. Capon finally took notice one day of me taking notice of that shot gun. He asked me if I was a hunter and of course I jumped at a no. I told him that my family and I were animal lovers. "Can I hold it?" I asked him. Mr. Capon gladly obliged and lifted that beautiful Stevens shot gun, my Stevens shotgun out of its case and handed it to me. I told him that I had never held a gun before. I tucked the butt into my shoulder and looked down the barrel.

Mr. Capon, who was an older gentleman, somebody's grandpa, chuckled as I held the shotgun. He told me that I was holding it all wrong and it would dislocate my shoulder if I fired it like that. My first lesson took place that day. The rifle was $125.00 and I was going to buy it.

Things work differently in a small town. We only had one town cop at that time and his name was Cody. He was very nice and elderly. Each time I saw him there would be a white chalky build up at the corners of his mouth from his calcium chews. Mr. Capon knew that I worked at the White Front Café and he also knew how much I wanted to buy that rifle. When he would come into the café on his coffee breaks, that rifle was all I talked about. It took me several months to save up enough money because I only made about $35 to $40 per pay check but after long while I finally had saved up enough. Mr. Capon said that I had to let Cody know I bought the shot gun, which I dutifully did. Cody never told me I needed a license, he never told me I needed to carry it in a case and said I could target shoot at the pits right outside of town. By the time I was able to buy the rifle, Mr. Capon had taught me how to hold it, proper hand placement, squeezing the trigger instead of pulling it and most importantly how to read the site. He even gave me my first box of shells for free. I handed him the money and he handed me my Stevens 12 gauge. I will never forget how excited I was to call it mine and carried it home, down Main Street to my house. Lanesboro was a sleepy town but there were always a few folks walking around or driving about. No one thought anything of it…a young teenage girl walking down the side walk carrying a shot gun, not even Cody. Now I needed to call Doug.

Doug was seventeen years old. He was one of my brother's buddies and I knew he would help me shoot. Doug was amused that I bought a shotgun instead of clothes, perfume or jewelry. He had five sisters and he was used to that. One nice summer day he and I met downtown and walked about two miles to the pits. My mother wasn't opposed to me buying a shot gun and she thought it was pretty too. She laughed and called me her little Annie Oakley. Mother trusted Doug and she was okay with us going out to target shoot. The anticipation of finally shooting my Stevens 12 gauge was almost more than I could handle. I wanted to run not walk. We just couldn't get there soon enough!

When we hit the 250 Bridge Doug led the way. We took a short cut over the rail road tracks and into the pits which was a place where there were mountains of sand that formed a barrier from the outside world. Doug was familiar with this place because there was an awesome and huge swimming hole. The pits were also a popular party spot for the local kids, because the area was secluded. Doug watched me check my site and load the shotgun. I have to admit, I took personal pride in showing off my new skills and I wanted him to be proud of me. He was like a brother. I tucked the butt into my shoulder and looked down the barrel to the row of empty Schmidt beer cans that Doug had set up about fifty meters away. I took a strong stance, dug my heels into the sand and braced myself. My heart was pounding out of my chest. I could hear Doug saying over and over "be ready for the kick, be ready for the kick". Then I inhaled and exhaled, paused for a second and squeezed the trigger, just like Mr. Capon had taught me.

My shot gun was louder than I thought it would be! It was powerful. All 106 pounds of me flew back on my rear end after the butt violently hit my right chin and jaw. It was lights out. The kick momentarily stunned me into submission. That was the first time I had ever gotten knocked out. I woke up to see Doug standing over me clutching his stomach and laughing hysterically (I guess it was his way of showing he cared). This only fueled my determination to jump up and shoot again, and again and again until we had finished the entire box of shot gun shells. It felt like my shoulder was dislocated and my jaw really hurt. I couldn't let Doug see my pain, I just couldn't because I didn't want him to think I was weak. It was a long walk home and it seemed to take forever. The smell of gun powder lingered the entire way. It excited me and put butterflies in my stomach, despite the pain. It was the same feeling I would get when smelling the exhaust from the school bus at the bus stop when I was little.

After turning seventeen I bought a 22 caliber Ruger from Mr. Capon. It was a pretty little shot gun and didn't kick like the 12 gauge or leave large bruises near my arm pit. It did have a difficult site and required more accurate firing. The Ruger also had a beautiful carving on its wooden butt and wasn't as expensive. This was the beginning of my gun collection. Later, after joining the army I would add a tiny little purse pistol to my collection when I was stationed at Ft. Ord, California. And several years later I bought a wickedly nice, foreign made 9 mm from a local national while passing through Prague (I was stationed in Germany). I loved my gun collection and my only motivation was to excel in my shooting skills. Frankly, I enjoyed the rush. I also learned to respect weapons and the power behind them. I can compare the feeling to be the same as when I would ride our sixteen hand high Saddlebred in a full gallop. It was a rush.

My shooting skills helped me excel in the Army Reserves, Regular Army and National Guard, thanks to Mr. Capon's many patient tutorials and my trips to the pits with Doug. I sold my guns after having children and haven't fired a weapon since my last year in the National Guard, which was back in 2011. I still have my target cards from the firing range at Camp Ripley and they live in the dust of my ten year military portfolio. When I was stationed at Ft. Bragg I had a caricature photo taken of me dressed like Annie Oakley and holding a rifle. She was one of my idols. I mailed the photo to mother and she got a kick out of it.

CONCLUSION

I live hours away from Lanesboro and haven't visited my hometown for several years. I doubt the pits are still there but my memories have made roots in the ground. Mr. Capon passed away years ago and his hardware store went with him. Doug is still a local and I am happy about that. Lanesboro is a changed world from my days as a child, teenager and young lady. My memories are vivid and sometimes can be very nostalgic. From my first day and into the first few years of living in Lanesboro, I never thought I could make the transition from an east coast city teenager to a small town Minnesota girl. I will say that I am incredibly proud to call Lanesboro my home. Its economic growth and the changes that have occurred over the past twenty five years are impressive. Lanesboro was listed in the Smithsonian magazine to be one of the top twenty bed and breakfast towns in America in 2015 and one of the top ten small town art places in America for the year 2013. Mrs. B's Inn was the founder for such a business. I remember her Bed & Breakfast to be one of the first in Lanesboro where she claimed the city corner at the end of the new bridge, laying the ground work for many more to come. The old St. Main theatre is quite famous now (Commonwealth Theatre) and it has been said to get close to twenty two thousand visitors annually. Crown Trout Jewelers are internationally known for their unique style, precious metals and beautiful stones. It is just an incredible fact, and to wrap my head around the idea that my teeny-tiny home town has become such a high dollar conglomerate of small businesses well, who would of thought?

Despite its transformation and huge popularity, I will forever see Lanesboro as it was; just a little farm town with hidden legacies, wonderful natural beauty and everlasting memories. We will always call the Oxtrail the Oxtrail and refer to Little Norway, up Brooklyn and the Flats as they were years ago. The Root River will always flow in the same direction and the many bridges will continue to hold their significant place in our memories. Johnny and Arnie Rank will be forever heroes and I would like to believe that their gentle spirits hover over their home town, our home town.

My big old house is still there and of course, is now a bed and breakfast. Thoen's Hotel is still just a few feet away and holds a legacy all of its own. If you listen real closely and use your imagination, you might be able to hear the old steam engine blow its horn as it passes over the railroad bridge and through Lanesboro as it did decades ago. For the many small business owners, (we used to call them out of towners) they will get a piece of the pie as Lanesboro has become one most visited small towns in America and with that, it has also become a gold mine. But the present and past Lanesboro Burros have more than what money can buy. We have our memories of Lanesboro's simpler times and lasting friendships that will never be broken. It was a good feeling when I knew who I was waving to while walking up town to Capons or down to the Flats to get an inner tube from Greg. Or whether it would be Dale walking down the street on his way back to his corner barber shop from having lunch at the White Front café, or Elton and Steve working at the filling station up Brooklyn with their never ending willingness to help anyone in need. And old Cody the town cop, who knew most everyone by name and let the kids be kids. I hold memories of my first Lefse and lutefisk feed at the legion where everyone knew each other and their children. I remember the warm laundromat in the winter time that Eva kept spotless, and the fact that she never fussed about youngsters jumping in to thaw for a minute and always had a smile on her face to welcome us (in fact, the main thing she was concerned about was that we weren't bundled up enough). And huddling up under the new bridge as teens sipping blackberry brandy to help fight the frigid winter wind on Sunday after a Vikings game. We liked to be outside, and even as youngsters we appreciated the beauty of our town in the middle of a winter snow.

I will never forget the many walks down to the flats to reach the pits for a swim or to fire my Steven's shotgun at a line of empty beer cans. The fun times I had snowmobiling with the country kids through the fields and the absolute silence of a fresh snow fall covering the town in a white blanket. By moving to Lanesboro I learned to respect nature and its inhabitants. I learned to appreciate the beauty of a freshly tilled field and the lovely smell of hay right after it had been cut and bailed. Little Norway will always hold significance in Lanesboro just by virtue of its name and will always make a great short-cut to the Oxtrail for a walk. I knew I would be exactly one mile out on my run when the Hanson farm would show up and about two miles out when the Benson's house revealed itself around the corner of the gravel road. I remember attending the high school bon fires at the football field right above the dam and the wooden look-out where you can safely get close enough to feel the mist and hear the roar of the water fall crashing down. Or spend Friday nights cruising up and down Main Street about a dozen times after a game; but mostly, being able to appreciate the wonders of an amazing and picturesque small mid-western farm town and the pride attached to it. I'm glad we moved from New York to Lanesboro so many years ago and I will forever call Lanesboro my home. Vivid memories take me back to seeing old Johnny Rank, with his tobacco stained beard and gentle eyes, creeping up the back ally and slowly shuffling down to the store determined to buy his cigarettes. And the grueling track practices that entailed running up and down the grade from the football field and back. I think I speak for most of Lanesboro's locals, young and old when I say we would take those days back it in a heartbeat. After all, home is where the heart is and my heart is in Lanesboro.

By the way, I must mention something in this book. Sally is a boy. I recently was enlightened by my older sibling that Sally was short for Salvatore. I don't think he minded being called Sally or rather Silly Sally and he was well loved by me, my family and friends.

Riding up Brooklyn (Top Left)
Melody and Heather's reunion ten years later (Top Right)
Melody holding her monkey Shawn (Bottom Left)
My sister, Lisa, holding Silly Sally (bottom right)

Mother holding Shawn with Mariah in the corral (Top Left)
Me and my sister in Port Jefferson, New York (Bottom Left)
My father on the east coast (Top Right)
Shawn in the camper (Bottom Right)

The Lanesboro Leader in the old days, turned Bed &
Breakfast - courtesy of Lanesboro (Top Left)
Big Ted (Bottom Left)
The house in 1979 (Top Right)
The dam/waterfall in the summer (Bottom Right)

Dear old Johnny Rank
(Above, Photo by Kate O'Neary)

My favorite flowered polyester shirt
(Above)

My crazy family

Some of my friends from
Lanesboro, cerca 1982

Printed in the United States
By Bookmasters